Soup Recipes

A Collection with Origins Included

Jacob Ward

Table of Contents

Introduction 7

Tomato Soup 8

Potato Leek Soup 9

Minestrone Soup 10

Cauliflower Soup 11

Chicken Noodle Soup 12

Lentil Soup 13

Tomato and Basil Soup 14

Cauliflower and Potato Soup 16

Carrot and Ginger Soup 17

Creamy Mushroom Soup 18

Split Pea Soup 19

Minestrone Soup with Chicken 20

Potato Soup 21

Spicy Black Bean Soup 22

Corn Chowder 23

Creamy Potato Leek Soup 24

Spicy Tomato Basil Soup 25

Gumbo Soup 26

Creamy Carrot Soup 28

Butternut Squash Soup 29

Creamy Broccoli Soup 31

Spicy Sweet Potato Soup 32

Chili Soup Recipe 33

Carrot Ginger Soup 35

Creamy Leek and Potato Soup 36

Spiced Sweet Potato Soup 37

Spicy Butternut Squash Soup 38

Creamy Zucchini Soup 40

French Onion Soup 41

Fish Soup 43

Crema Parmentier 44

Chicken and Rice Soup 45

Creamy Prawn Soup 47

Avgolemono Soup Recipe 48

Borscht Soup Recipe 49

Bouillabaisse Soup Recipe 51

Cullen Skink Soup 52

Erwtensoep (Dutch Pea Soup) 53

Creamy Potato Soup 55

Escarole Soup 56

Pea Soup 57

Beet and Coconut Soup 58

West Coast Clam Chowder 59

Vegetable Soup 60

Mushroom Barley Soup 61

Chicken and Dumpling Stew 62

Zuppa di Tortellini 63

Spinach and Chickpea Soup 64

East Coast Clam Chowder 66

Pumpkin Stew 67

Matzo Ball Stew 68

Beef Pho Soup 69

Beer and Cheddar Soup 71

Potato and Spicy Shrimp Stew 72

Crab Bisque 73

Beet and Tomato Soup 75

Potato and Asparagus Soup 76

Oyster Stew 77

Green Chili Pork Stew 78

Cheeseburger Soup 79

Buffalo Chicken Soup 81

Sweet Potato Chowder 82

Spinach Bisque 83

Chicken Gumbo Soup 85

Chicken Ravioli Soup 86

Hearty Cabbage Soup 87

Sweet and Savory Corn Soup 88

Easy Tomato Gnocchi Soup 89

Roasted Pepper Soup 90

Ginger Apple Carrot Soup 91

Coconut Pumpkin Soup 93

Creamy Celery Soup 94

Tuscan Chicken Soup 95

Polish Chicken Broth 96

Chicken Lentil Soup 97

California Vegetable Medley Soup 99

Mediterranean Vegetable Soup 100

North African Vegetable Soup 101

Indonesian Crab Soup 102

Pure Texas Beef Chili Soup 104

New England Clam Chowder 105

Gazpacho Soup 106

Tom Yum Soup Recipe 107

Maryland Crab Chowder Recipe 109

Rouille Recipe 110

Vietnamese Pho with Beef Recipe 111

Sauerkraut Soup Recipe 112

Pearl Barley Soup Recipe 113

Conclusion 114

Welcome to our soup cookbook! Here, you'll find a collection of delicious and comforting soups to warm you up on chilly days. From classic vegetable soup to hearty chili and everything in between, there's something for everyone in this book. Every recipe is accompanied by the description of the soup's origin. So, grab a spoon and let's get started on a delicious culinary journey through the world of soups.

Soups are healthy and good because:

1. Hydrating: Most soups contain a high amount of water, making them a great source of hydration.
2. Nutritious: Soups can be made with a variety of nutritious ingredients, such as vegetables, legumes, and lean proteins.
3. Easy to digest: The liquid consistency of soups makes them easy to digest, making them a good option for those with digestive issues.
4. Versatile: Soups can be made with a wide range of ingredients, allowing for a variety of flavor options and the ability to incorporate a diverse range of nutrients into one meal.
5. Filling: Soups can be filling due to the high water content and the inclusion of filling ingredients such as carbohydrates and proteins.

Tomato Soup

Ingredients:

- 2 lbs of ripe tomatoes
- 1 onion, diced
- 2 cloves of garlic, minced
- 1 tablespoon of olive oil
- 2 cups of vegetable broth
- Salt and pepper to taste
- Fresh basil leaves for garnish

Instructions:

1. Heat olive oil in a large pot over medium heat.
2. Add the diced onions and minced garlic and cook until softened, about 3-5 minutes.
3. Cut the tomatoes in half, squeeze out the seeds, and chop into large pieces. Add to the pot.
4. Pour in the vegetable broth and bring to a boil. Reduce heat and let simmer for 10 minutes.
5. Use an immersion blender or transfer the mixture to a blender and blend until smooth.
6. Season with salt and pepper to taste.
7. Serve hot, garnished with fresh basil leaves.

Note: The origin of tomato soup is uncertain, but it is believed to have been popularized in America in the late 19th century.

Ingredients:

- 3 medium leeks
- 4 large potatoes, peeled and diced
- 2 tablespoons of butter
- 4 cups of chicken or vegetable broth
- Salt and pepper to taste
- Chives for garnish

Instructions:

1. Clean and slice the leeks, discarding the tough green parts.
2. In a large pot, melt the butter over medium heat.
3. Add the sliced leeks and cook until softened, about 5 minutes.
4. Add the diced potatoes and broth to the pot.
5. Bring to a boil, then reduce heat and let simmer for 15-20 minutes, or until the potatoes are tender.
6. Use an immersion blender or transfer the mixture to a blender and blend until smooth.
7. Season with salt and pepper to taste.
8. Serve hot, garnished with chopped chives.

Note: Potato leek soup is a traditional French soup.

Minestrone Soup

Ingredients:

- 2 tablespoons of olive oil
- 1 onion, diced
- 2 cloves of garlic, minced
- 2 carrots, chopped
- 2 stalks of celery, chopped
- 2 cans of diced tomatoes
- 2 cups of vegetable broth
- 1 can of kidney beans, drained and rinsed
- 1 cup of small pasta, such as ditalini
- Salt and pepper to taste
- Fresh basil leaves for garnish

Instructions:

1. Heat olive oil in a large pot over medium heat.
2. Add the diced onion and minced garlic and cook until softened, about 3-5 minutes.
3. Add the chopped carrots and celery and cook for another 5 minutes.
4. Pour in the diced tomatoes and vegetable broth. Bring to a boil, then reduce heat and let simmer for 10 minutes.
5. Stir in the kidney beans and pasta. Let cook for an additional 10 minutes, or until the pasta is tender.

6. Season with salt and pepper to taste.

7. Serve hot, garnished with fresh basil leaves.

Note: Minestrone soup is a traditional Italian soup that originated in the Tuscan region of Italy.

Cauliflower Soup

Ingredients:

- 1 head of cauliflower, chopped
- 1 onion, diced
- 2 cloves of garlic, minced
- 2 tablespoons of butter
- 4 cups of chicken or vegetable broth
- Salt and pepper to taste
- Fresh parsley for garnish

Instructions:

1. In a large pot, melt the butter over medium heat.

2. Add the diced onion and minced garlic and cook until softened, about 3-5 minutes.

3. Add the chopped cauliflower to the pot and cook for another 5 minutes.

4. Pour in the broth and bring to a boil. Reduce heat and let simmer for 15-20 minutes, or until the cauliflower is tender.
5. Use an immersion blender or transfer the mixture to a blender and blend until smooth.
6. Season with salt and pepper to taste.
7. Serve hot, garnished with fresh parsley.

Note: The origin of cauliflower soup is uncertain, but it has become a popular soup in many countries.

Chicken Noodle Soup

Ingredients:

- 1 rotisserie chicken, shredded
- 1 onion, diced
- 2 carrots, chopped
- 2 stalks of celery, chopped
- 2 cloves of garlic, minced
- 8 cups of chicken broth
- 1 cup of egg noodles
- Salt and pepper to taste
- Fresh parsley for garnish

Instructions:

1. In a large pot, add the diced onion, chopped carrots, celery, and minced garlic. Cook until softened, about 5 minutes.
2. Pour in the chicken broth and bring to a boil.
3. Stir in the egg noodles and cook for 8-10 minutes, or until tender.
4. Add the shredded rotisserie chicken to the pot and let heat through, about 5 minutes.
5. Season with salt and pepper to taste.
6. Serve hot, garnished with fresh parsley.

Note: Chicken noodle soup is a classic comfort soup that has been enjoyed for generations. It is believed to have originated in Europe and has since become popular in many countries around the world.

Lentil Soup

Ingredients:

- 1 cup of lentils
- 1 onion, diced
- 2 carrots, chopped
- 2 stalks of celery, chopped
- 2 cloves of garlic, minced
- 6 cups of vegetable broth

- 1 can of diced tomatoes
- Salt and pepper to taste
- Fresh parsley for garnish

Instructions:

1. Rinse the lentils and pick out any small stones or debris.
2. In a large pot, add the diced onion, chopped carrots, celery, and minced garlic. Cook until softened, about 5 minutes.
3. Stir in the lentils, vegetable broth, and diced tomatoes.
4. Bring to a boil, then reduce heat and let simmer for 30-35 minutes, or until the lentils are tender.
5. Use an immersion blender or transfer the mixture to a blender and blend until slightly chunky.
6. Season with salt and pepper to taste.
7. Serve hot, garnished with fresh parsley.

Note: Lentil soup is a staple in many cultures, particularly in the Middle East and Mediterranean regions. It is a nutritious and filling soup that is easy to make and full of flavor.

Tomato and Basil Soup

Ingredients:

- 4 medium sized ripe tomatoes

- 2 cloves of garlic
- 1 onion, chopped
- 2 tbsp olive oil
- 2 tbsp fresh basil, chopped
- Salt and pepper, to taste
- 4 cups vegetable broth
- 1 cup heavy cream (optional)

Instructions:

1. In a large pot, heat the olive oil over medium heat.
2. Add the onion and garlic and cook until softened, about 5 minutes.
3. Add the chopped tomatoes, vegetable broth, salt, and pepper.
4. Bring to a boil, then reduce heat and let simmer for 10 minutes.
5. Remove from heat and add the chopped basil.
6. Blend the mixture until smooth.
7. Return the soup to the pot and stir in the heavy cream, if using.
8. Reheat the soup and serve.

This soup originates from Italy and is a classic summer dish, often made with fresh, ripe tomatoes.

Ingredients:

- 1 head of cauliflower, chopped
- 2 large potatoes, peeled and chopped
- 1 onion, chopped
- 2 tbsp butter
- 4 cups chicken or vegetable broth
- 1 cup heavy cream
- Salt and pepper, to taste

Instructions:

1. In a large pot, melt the butter over medium heat.
2. Add the onion and cook until softened, about 5 minutes.
3. Add the chopped cauliflower and potatoes, salt, and pepper.
4. Pour in the broth and bring to a boil.
5. Reduce heat and let simmer until the vegetables are soft, about 15-20 minutes.
6. Remove from heat and blend the mixture until smooth.
7. Return the soup to the pot and stir in the heavy cream.
8. Reheat the soup and serve.

This soup originates from England and is a hearty, comforting dish that is perfect for cold weather.

Ingredients:

- 4 medium sized carrots, peeled and chopped
- 1 large piece of fresh ginger, peeled and grated
- 1 onion, chopped
- 2 tbsp olive oil
- 4 cups vegetable broth
- Salt and pepper, to taste

Instructions:

1. In a large pot, heat the olive oil over medium heat.
2. Add the onion and cook until softened, about 5 minutes.
3. Add the chopped carrots, grated ginger, salt, and pepper.
4. Pour in the vegetable broth and bring to a boil.
5. Reduce heat and let simmer until the carrots are soft, about 15-20 minutes.
6. Remove from heat and blend the mixture until smooth.
7. Return the soup to the pot and reheat.
8. Serve hot.

This soup originates from Asia and is a flavorful, healthy dish that is perfect for a light meal or as a starter.

Creamy Mushroom Soup

Ingredients:

- 1 lb. mushrooms, sliced
- 1 onion, chopped
- 3 cloves of garlic, minced
- 4 tbsp butter
- 4 cups chicken or vegetable broth
- 1 cup heavy cream
- Salt and pepper, to taste

Instructions:

1. In a large pot, melt the butter over medium heat.
2. Add the onion and garlic and cook until softened, about 5 minutes.
3. Add the sliced mushrooms, salt, and pepper.
4. Cook for another 5 minutes, or until the mushrooms are tender.
5. Pour in the broth and bring to a boil.
6. Reduce heat and let simmer for 10 minutes.
7. Remove from heat and blend the mixture until smooth.
8. Return the soup to the pot and stir in the heavy cream.
9. Reheat the soup and serve.

This soup is a classic dish that can be found in many countries, including France and the United States.

Split Pea Soup

Ingredients:

- 1 lb. green split peas
- 1 ham hock or 1 cup diced ham
- 1 onion, chopped
- 3 cloves of garlic, minced
- 2 tbsp olive oil
- 6 cups chicken or vegetable broth
- Salt and pepper, to taste

Instructions:

1. In a large pot, heat the olive oil over medium heat.
2. Add the onion and garlic and cook until softened, about 5 minutes.
3. Add the split peas, diced ham (or ham hock), salt, and pepper.
4. Pour in the broth and bring to a boil.
5. Reduce heat and let simmer until the peas are soft, about 1 hour.
6. Remove the ham hock (if using) and let cool.
7. Remove the meat from the ham hock and chop.
8. Return the meat to the soup and reheat.
9. Serve hot.

This soup originates from England and is a traditional dish that is often served with crusty bread

Ingredients:

- 1 can of diced tomatoes
- 1 cup carrots, chopped
- 1 cup celery, chopped
- 1 cup onion, chopped
- 3 cloves of garlic, minced
- 2 tbsp olive oil
- 4 cups chicken or vegetable broth
- 1 cup small pasta such as ditalini or elbow macaroni
- 1 cup kidney or cannellini beans
- 1 cup frozen green beans or peas
- Salt and pepper, to taste

Instructions:

1. In a large pot, heat the olive oil over medium heat.
2. Add the onion, carrots, celery, and garlic and cook until softened, about 5 minutes.
3. Add the canned tomatoes, broth, pasta, beans, green beans/peas, salt, and pepper.
4. Bring to a boil, then reduce heat and let simmer for 15-20 minutes.
5. Serve hot.

This soup originates from Italy and is a classic, hearty dish often made with whatever vegetables are in season

Potato Soup

Ingredients:

- 2 lbs. potatoes, peeled and chopped
- 1 onion, chopped
- 3 cloves of garlic, minced
- 2 tbsp butter
- 4 cups chicken or vegetable broth
- 1 cup heavy cream (optional)
- Salt and pepper, to taste

Instructions:

1. In a large pot, melt the butter over medium heat.
2. Add the onion and garlic and cook until softened, about 5 minutes.
3. Add the chopped potatoes, salt, and pepper.
4. Pour in the broth and bring to a boil.
5. Reduce heat and let simmer until the potatoes are soft, about 15-20 minutes.
6. Remove from heat and blend the mixture until smooth.
7. Return the soup to the pot and stir in the heavy cream, if using.
8. Reheat the soup and serve.

Potato soup is a hearty and filling dish that is popular in many countries, including Ireland and Germany. It can be served as a main course or as a starter.

Ingredients:

- 1 lb. dried black beans, soaked overnight
- 1 onion, chopped
- 3 cloves of garlic, minced
- 2 tbsp olive oil
- 4 cups chicken or vegetable broth
- 2 tbsp chili powder
- 1 tsp cumin
- 1 tsp paprika
- Salt and pepper, to taste
- Sour cream and cilantro, for serving (optional)

Instructions:

1. In a large pot, heat the olive oil over medium heat.
2. Add the onion and garlic and cook until softened, about 5 minutes.
3. Add the chili powder, cumin, paprika, salt, and pepper.
4. Pour in the broth and black beans.
5. Bring to a boil, then reduce heat and let simmer until the beans are tender, about 1 hour.
6. Remove from heat and blend the mixture until smooth.
7. Return the soup to the pot and reheat.

8. Serve hot with a dollop of sour cream and a sprinkle of cilantro, if desired.

Spicy black bean soup is a staple in many Latin American countries, especially Mexico. It is a hearty and flavorful dish that is often enjoyed with rice or tortillas.

Corn Chowder

Ingredients:

- 4 ears of corn, kernels removed
- 1 onion, chopped
- 3 cloves of garlic, minced
- 2 tbsp butter
- 4 cups chicken or vegetable broth
- 1 cup heavy cream
- Salt and pepper, to taste

Instructions:

1. In a large pot, melt the butter over medium heat.
2. Add the onion and garlic and cook until softened, about 5 minutes.
3. Add the corn kernels, salt, and pepper.
4. Pour in the broth and bring to a boil.

5. Reduce heat and let simmer for 10 minutes.

6. Remove from heat and blend the mixture until smooth.

7. Return the soup to the pot and stir in the heavy cream.

8. Reheat the soup and serve.

Corn chowder is a classic American dish that is popular in many regions, especially in New England. It is a creamy and flavorful soup that is often served with crusty bread or crackers.

Creamy Potato Leek Soup

Ingredients:

- 4 medium potatoes, peeled and diced
- 2 large leeks, sliced
- 4 cups chicken or vegetable broth
- 1 cup heavy cream
- Salt and pepper to taste

Instructions:

1. In a large pot, saute the sliced leeks over medium heat until softened, about 5 minutes.

2. Add the diced potatoes and broth to the pot and bring to a boil.

3. Reduce heat to low and simmer until the potatoes are tender, about 20 minutes.

4. Remove from heat and let cool slightly.

5. Puree the soup in a blender or with an immersion blender until smooth.

6. Return the pureed soup to the pot and stir in the heavy cream.

7. Season with salt and pepper to taste.

8. Reheat the soup over low heat until warmed through, about 5 minutes.

Soup is a staple of many cultures and is believed to have originated in ancient civilizations. The use of potatoes and leeks in this soup is commonly associated with French cuisine, where the combination is known as "potage parmentier."

Spicy Tomato Basil Soup

Ingredients:

- 1 large onion, chopped
- 2 cloves garlic, minced
- 2 cans diced tomatoes
- 4 cups chicken or vegetable broth
- 1/2 teaspoon red pepper flakes
- Salt and pepper to taste
- 1/4 cup fresh basil, chopped

Instructions:

1. In a large pot, saute the chopped onion and minced garlic over medium heat until softened, about 5 minutes.
2. Add the diced tomatoes, broth, red pepper flakes, salt, and pepper to the pot.
3. Bring to a boil, then reduce heat to low and simmer for 15 minutes.
4. Remove from heat and let cool slightly.
5. Puree the soup in a blender or with an immersion blender until smooth.
6. Stir in the chopped basil.
7. Reheat the soup over low heat until warmed through, about 5 minutes.

Tomato soup is a classic and beloved soup in many countries. The addition of spicy red pepper flakes and fresh basil in this recipe gives it a touch of Italian flavor.

Gumbo Soup

Ingredients:

- 2 tbsp vegetable oil
- 1 large onion, chopped
- 1 green bell pepper, chopped

- 1 stalk celery, chopped
- 2 cloves garlic, minced
- 2 cups chicken broth
- 1 can diced tomatoes
- 1 cup sliced okra
- 1 cup sliced Andouille sausage
- 2 tbsp flour
- Salt and pepper to taste

Instructions:

1. Heat the vegetable oil in a large saucepan over medium heat.
2. Add the onion, bell pepper, celery and garlic, and cook until softened, about 5 minutes.
3. Stir in the flour, and cook for 2-3 minutes until the flour is lightly browned.
4. Pour in the chicken broth, tomatoes, okra and Andouille sausage.
5. Bring the mixture to a boil and then reduce heat to low.
6. Simmer for 15-20 minutes, or until the vegetables are tender.
7. Season with salt and pepper to taste.

Gumbo is a traditional soup from Louisiana, USA, and is a staple of Cajun and Creole cuisine.

Ingredients:

- 4 medium sized carrots, chopped
- 1 large onion, chopped
- 4 cloves of garlic, minced
- 4 cups of vegetable broth
- 1 cup of heavy cream
- 2 tablespoons of butter
- Salt and pepper, to taste
- Fresh parsley for garnish (optional)

Instructions:

1. In a large pot, melt the butter over medium heat. Add the chopped onions and minced garlic, and sauté until the onions are translucent.
2. Add the chopped carrots and sauté for another 2-3 minutes.
3. Pour in the vegetable broth and bring to a boil. Reduce heat to low and let simmer for 15-20 minutes or until the carrots are soft.
4. Remove the pot from heat and let cool slightly.
5. Blend the soup in a blender until smooth.
6. Pour the blended soup back into the pot and stir in the heavy cream.
7. Season with salt and pepper to taste.

8. Reheat the soup over low heat until hot.

9. Serve hot, garnished with fresh parsley if desired.

Origins: This creamy carrot soup is a classic soup originating in Europe. It is a comforting and easy to make soup that can be enjoyed any time of the year.

Butternut Squash Soup

Ingredients:

- 1 large butternut squash, peeled, seeded, and chopped
- 1 large onion, chopped
- 4 cloves of garlic, minced
- 4 cups of chicken broth
- 1 teaspoon of dried thyme
- 1 teaspoon of dried rosemary
- Salt and pepper, to taste
- 1 cup of heavy cream
- 2 tablespoons of butter
- Fresh parsley for garnish (optional)

Instructions:

1. In a large pot, melt the butter over medium heat. Add the chopped onions and minced garlic, and sauté until the onions are translucent.
2. Add the chopped butternut squash and sauté for another 2-3 minutes.
3. Pour in the chicken broth and bring to a boil. Reduce heat to low and let simmer for 15-20 minutes or until the butternut squash is soft.
4. Remove the pot from heat and let cool slightly.
5. Blend the soup in a blender until smooth.
6. Pour the blended soup back into the pot and stir in the heavy cream.
7. Season with thyme, rosemary, salt, and pepper to taste.
8. Reheat the soup over low heat until hot.
9. Serve hot, garnished with fresh parsley if desired.

Origins: Butternut Squash Soup is a popular North American soup. The butternut squash is native to North America and has been used in soups for centuries.

Ingredients:

- 2 tbsp butter
- 1 large onion, diced
- 3 cloves garlic, minced
- 4 cups broccoli florets
- 4 cups chicken or vegetable broth
- 1 cup heavy cream
- Salt and pepper to taste
- Shredded cheddar cheese, for garnish (optional)

Instructions:

1. In a large pot, melt the butter over medium heat. Add the onion and garlic and cook until softened, about 5 minutes.
2. Stir in the broccoli and broth. Bring to a boil and then reduce heat to low and simmer for 20 minutes, or until the broccoli is tender.
3. Remove from heat and use an immersion blender or blend in a blender in batches until smooth.
4. Return the soup to the pot and stir in the cream. Season with salt and pepper to taste.
5. Serve hot and garnish with shredded cheddar cheese, if desired.

The origin of Creamy Broccoli Soup is not clear, but it is believed to have originated in the United States in the mid-20th century as a way to use up surplus broccoli. It became popular as a hearty and healthy comfort food, and variations of the dish can now be found around the world.

Spicy Sweet Potato Soup

Ingredients:

- 2 tbsp olive oil
- 1 large onion, chopped
- 3 garlic cloves, minced
- 2 lbs sweet potatoes, peeled and chopped
- 4 cups chicken or vegetable broth
- 1 cup water
- 1 tsp ground cumin
- 1 tsp chili powder
- Salt and pepper to taste
- Sour cream, for garnish (optional)

Instructions:

1. In a large pot, heat the oil over medium heat. Add the onion and garlic and cook until softened, about 5 minutes.
2. Stir in the sweet potatoes, broth, water, cumin, and chili powder. Bring to a boil and then reduce heat to low and simmer for 20 minutes, or until the sweet potatoes are tender.

3. Use an immersion blender or blend in a blender in batches until smooth.

4. Season with salt and pepper to taste.

5. Serve hot and garnish with sour cream, if desired.

Soup has been a staple food for centuries and its origins can be traced back to early human civilizations. The combination of easily accessible ingredients and the ability to feed a large number of people with one pot of soup made it a popular choice for meals. Over time, various cultures have developed their own unique soup recipes, showcasing the dish's versatility and adaptability.

Chili Soup Recipe

Ingredients:

- 1 lb ground beef or turkey
- 1 onion, chopped
- 2 cloves of garlic, minced
- 1 red bell pepper, chopped
- 2 tablespoons chili powder
- 1 teaspoon cumin
- 1 teaspoon dried oregano
- 1 can of diced tomatoes
- 1 can of red kidney beans, drained and rinsed
- 4 cups of beef or chicken broth

- Salt and pepper to taste

Instructions:

1. In a large pot, heat a tablespoon of oil over medium heat. Add the ground beef and cook until browned, about 5 minutes.
2. Add the onion, garlic, and red bell pepper to the pot and cook for 5 minutes, until softened.
3. Stir in the chili powder, cumin, and oregano, and cook for another minute.
4. Pour in the diced tomatoes, red kidney beans, and broth. Stir to combine.
5. Bring the mixture to a boil, then reduce heat to low, cover, and simmer for 20-30 minutes.
6. Season with salt and pepper to taste. Serve with toppings of your choice, such as shredded cheese, sour cream, diced avocado, or cilantro.

Chili soup originates from the Southwest region of the United States, with roots in Mexican and Tex-Mex cuisine. The dish typically combines chili spices and ground beef with beans, tomatoes, and other ingredients to create a hearty, warming soup. Variations of chili soup can be found in other countries and regions, such as India and Thailand, often incorporating local ingredients and spices.

Ingredients:

- 1 tbsp olive oil
- 1 onion, chopped
- 2 garlic cloves, minced
- 2 lbs carrots, peeled and chopped
- 2 inch piece of ginger, peeled and grated
- 4 cups vegetable broth
- 1 tsp salt
- 1 tsp black pepper
- 1 cup heavy cream
- 2 tbsp chopped fresh parsley

Instructions:

1. Heat the oil in a large pot over medium heat.
2. Add the onion and garlic and cook until softened, about 5 minutes.
3. Stir in the chopped carrots and grated ginger, cook for 2-3 minutes.
4. Pour in the vegetable broth, salt and pepper, bring to a boil.
5. Reduce heat and let it simmer until the carrots are tender, about 20 minutes.
6. Remove from heat and use an immersion blender or transfer to a blender to puree the soup until smooth.

7.   Stir in the heavy cream and heat through.

8.   Serve in bowls and garnish with fresh parsley.

This soup is believed to have originated in Southeast Asia and has since become popular worldwide.

Creamy Leek and Potato Soup

Ingredients:

- 2 tbsp butter
- 2 lbs leeks, white and light green parts only, sliced
- 2 lbs potatoes, peeled and diced
- 4 cups chicken or vegetable broth
- 1 tsp salt
- 1 tsp black pepper
- 1 cup heavy cream
- 2 tbsp chopped fresh chives

Instructions:

1.   Melt the butter in a large pot over medium heat.

2.   Add the sliced leeks and cook until soft and translucent, about 5 minutes.

3.   Stir in the diced potatoes, broth, salt and pepper, bring to a boil.

4. Reduce heat and let it simmer until the potatoes are tender, about 20 minutes.
5. Remove from heat and use an immersion blender or transfer to a blender to puree the soup until smooth.
6. Stir in the heavy cream and heat through.
7. Serve in bowls and garnish with fresh chives.

This soup is believed to have originated in the UK and has since become popular worldwide.

Spiced Sweet Potato Soup

Ingredients:

- 2 tbsp olive oil
- 1 onion, chopped
- 2 garlic cloves, minced
- 2 lbs sweet potatoes, peeled and chopped
- 2 tsp ground cumin
- 2 tsp ground coriander
- 4 cups chicken or vegetable broth
- 1 tsp salt
- 1 tsp black pepper
- 1 cup heavy cream

- 2 tbsp chopped fresh cilantro

Instructions:

1. Heat the oil in a large pot over medium heat.
2. Add the onion and garlic and cook until softened, about 5 minutes.
3. Stir in the chopped sweet potatoes, cumin, coriander, broth, salt and pepper, bring to a boil.
4. Reduce heat and let it simmer until the sweet potatoes are tender, about 20 minutes.
5. Remove from heat and use an immersion blender or transfer to a blender to puree the soup until smooth.
6. Stir in the heavy cream and heat through.
7. Serve in bowls and garnish with fresh cilantro.

This soup is believed to have originated in Africa and has since become popular worldwide, particularly in Caribbean cuisine.

Spicy Butternut Squash Soup

Ingredients:

- 1 tablespoon olive oil
- 1 onion, chopped

- 3 cloves garlic, minced
- 2 lbs butternut squash, peeled, seeded, and chopped
- 4 cups chicken or vegetable broth
- 1 can of diced tomatoes
- 1 teaspoon cumin
- 1 teaspoon chili powder
- Salt and pepper, to taste
- Heavy cream or sour cream, for serving (optional)

Instructions:

1. Heat the olive oil in a large pot over medium heat.
2. Add the onion and garlic, and cook until the onion is soft and translucent, about 5 minutes.
3. Add the chopped butternut squash, cumin, and chili powder, and cook for another 5 minutes.
4. Pour in the chicken or vegetable broth and diced tomatoes and bring to a boil.
5. Reduce the heat and let the soup simmer until the squash is tender, about 15 minutes.
6. Use an immersion blender or transfer the soup to a blender and blend until smooth.
7. Season the soup with salt and pepper to taste.

The origin of Spicy Butternut Squash Soup is unclear and varies in different regions. However, the dish is commonly attributed to the use of butternut squash, a versatile vegetable that has been used in cooking for centuries, combined with spices and other ingredients to create a warm, comforting soup.

Creamy Zucchini Soup

Ingredients:

- 2 lbs zucchini, chopped
- 1 large onion, chopped
- 4 cloves garlic, minced
- 4 cups chicken or vegetable broth
- 1 cup heavy cream
- Salt and pepper to taste

Instructions:

1. In a large pot, saute the onions and garlic over medium heat until softened.
2. Add the chopped zucchini and broth and bring to a boil.
3. Reduce heat to low and let simmer for 10 minutes or until the zucchini is soft.

4. Remove from heat and let cool for a few minutes.

5. Blend the soup with a hand-held blender or transfer to a blender and puree until smooth.

6. Return the pureed soup to the pot and add the heavy cream, salt and pepper.

7. Reheat the soup until heated through and serve.

The origin of Creamy Zucchini Soup is uncertain, but it is believed to have originated in Mediterranean cuisine, where zucchini is a commonly used ingredient. Over time, variations of the dish have been developed in different regions and cultures, leading to the creamy version that is popular today.

French Onion Soup

Ingredients:

- 2 lbs yellow onions, sliced
- 4 tbsp unsalted butter
- 2 cups beef broth
- 2 cups chicken broth
- 1 cup red wine
- 1 tbsp thyme
- Salt and pepper to taste

- 4 slices French bread

- 4 oz Gruyere cheese, grated

1. In a large pot, melt the butter over medium heat and add the sliced onions.
2. Cook the onions until they are soft and caramelized, about 30 minutes.
3. Add the broths, wine, thyme, salt, and pepper and bring to a boil.
4. Reduce heat to low and let simmer for 20 minutes.
5. Preheat oven to 400°F.
6. Ladle the soup into oven-safe bowls and top each bowl with a slice of bread.
7. Sprinkle the grated cheese over the bread and place the bowls on a baking sheet.
8. Bake in the oven for 10-15 minutes or until the cheese is melted and bubbly.

The origin of French Onion Soup can be traced back to ancient Roman times, where it was made with onions, wine, and cheese. Over time, it evolved into the classic French dish we know today, with a rich broth made from caramelized onions and beef stock, topped with a slice of bread and melted cheese. The dish is thought to have become popular in France in the 17th century and became a staple in French bistros and cafes.

Ingredients:

- 1 lb fish fillets, cut into bite-sized pieces
- 2 tbsp olive oil
- 1 large onion, chopped
- 4 cloves garlic, minced
- 4 cups fish broth
- 2 cups chopped tomatoes
- 2 tbsp tomato paste
- 1 tsp dried thyme
- Salt and pepper to taste
- 2 tbsp chopped fresh parsley for garnish

Instructions:

1. In a large pot, heat the olive oil over medium heat and add the onion and garlic.
2. Cook until softened, about 5 minutes.
3. Add the broth, tomatoes, tomato paste, thyme, salt, and pepper and bring to a boil.
4. Reduce heat to low and let simmer for 10 minutes.
5. Add the fish fillets to the pot and let cook for 5 minutes or until the fish is cooked through.
6. Serve the soup hot and garnished with fresh parsley.

Note: The origin of fish soup is unknown but it is commonly enjoyed in many coastal regions around the world. Fish soup recipes vary greatly depending on the region and the type of fish used.

Crema Parmentier

Ingredients:

- 2 medium potatoes, peeled and diced
- 1 onion, chopped
- 3 cloves of garlic, minced
- 3 cups of chicken or vegetable broth
- 1 cup of heavy cream
- Salt and pepper to taste
- Fresh parsley or chives for garnish

Instructions:

1. In a large pot, cook the diced potatoes and chopped onion in the chicken or vegetable broth until the potatoes are soft and the onion is translucent.
2. Add in the minced garlic and continue to cook for another minute.
3. Use an immersion blender or transfer the mixture to a blender and puree until smooth.

4. Pour the pureed mixture back into the pot, add the heavy cream and bring to a simmer.

5. Season with salt and pepper to taste.

6. Serve hot, garnished with fresh parsley or chives.

The origin of the Crema Parmentier soup is believed to be French. It is named after Antoine-Augustin Parmentier, a French agronomist and nutritionist who promoted the cultivation and consumption of potatoes in France in the 18th century. The soup is typically made with potatoes, leeks, and cream, and is a classic example of French cuisine.

Chicken and Rice Soup

Ingredients:

- 1 large onion, chopped
- 2 carrots, diced
- 2 celery stalks, diced
- 3 cloves of garlic, minced
- 8 cups of chicken broth
- 1 cup of uncooked white rice
- 1 pound boneless chicken breasts, cut into bite-sized pieces

- Salt and pepper to taste
- Fresh parsley for garnish

Instructions:

1. In a large pot, cook the chopped onion, diced carrots, and diced celery until the onion is translucent.
2. Add in the minced garlic and continue to cook for another minute.
3. Pour in the chicken broth, bring to a simmer, and then add the uncooked white rice.
4. Add in the chicken pieces and cook until the chicken is cooked through and the rice is tender, about 20-25 minutes.
5. Season with salt and pepper to taste.
6. Serve hot, garnished with fresh parsley.

The origin of Chicken and Rice Soup is not clear and could have been created in various cultures and countries. However, it is a classic comfort food that has been enjoyed worldwide for centuries and is often considered a staple in many households. The soup typically consists of chicken, rice, and vegetables simmered in a flavorful broth and is often served as a comforting and hearty meal.

Ingredients:

- 1 onion, chopped
- 2 cloves of garlic, minced
- 1 tablespoon of butter
- 2 cups of chicken or vegetable broth
- 1 cup of heavy cream
- 1 pound of cooked prawns, peeled and deveined
- Salt and pepper to taste
- Fresh parsley for garnish

Instructions:

1. In a large pot, cook the chopped onion and minced garlic in the butter until the onion is translucent.
2. Pour in the chicken or vegetable broth and bring to a simmer.
3. Add in the cooked prawns and continue to cook for another 5 minutes.
4. Use an immersion blender or transfer the mixture to a blender and puree until smooth.
5. Pour the pureed mixture back into the pot, add the heavy cream and bring to a simmer.
6. Season with salt and pepper to taste.
7. Serve hot, garnished with fresh parsley.

The origin of the Creamy Prawn Soup is not clear and could have various regional or cultural roots. It is likely that this soup is inspired by the classic French or Italian seafood soups and stews which have been adapted and modified over time to create unique and varied dishes in different regions. The addition of cream is a common ingredient to add richness and smoothness to seafood soups.

Avgolemono Soup Recipe

Ingredients:

- 4 cups chicken broth
- 2 cups cooked, shredded chicken
- 2 eggs
- 2 lemons, juiced
- 2 tbsp cornstarch
- Salt and pepper, to taste

Instructions:

1. In a medium saucepan, bring chicken broth to a boil over medium heat.
2. In a separate bowl, whisk together the eggs, lemon juice, and cornstarch.

3. Slowly pour a cup of the hot broth into the egg mixture while whisking continuously.

4. Pour the egg mixture back into the saucepan with the remaining broth.

5. Add the shredded chicken to the soup and stir.

6. Cook over low heat, stirring constantly, until the soup thickens, about 5 minutes.

7. Season with salt and pepper to taste.

8. Serve hot.

Avgolemono is a traditional Greek soup made with chicken broth, eggs, and lemon juice. The word "Avgolemono" comes from the Greek words "Avgo" meaning egg and "lemoni" meaning lemon. It is a creamy and comforting soup, often served as a main course or with rice.

Borscht Soup Recipe

Ingredients:

- 2 tbsp olive oil
- 1 large onion, diced
- 2 large carrots, peeled and diced
- 2 large beets, peeled and diced
- 4 cups vegetable broth

- 2 cups shredded cabbage
- 1 can diced tomatoes
- 2 tbsp white wine vinegar
- 2 tsp sugar
- Salt and pepper, to taste

Instructions:

1. In a large soup pot, heat the olive oil over medium heat.
2. Add the diced onion, carrots, and beets, and cook until softened, about 10 minutes.
3. Add the vegetable broth, shredded cabbage, diced tomatoes, white wine vinegar, and sugar.
4. Bring the soup to a boil, then reduce heat and let it simmer for 20 minutes.
5. Season with salt and pepper to taste.
6. Serve hot with a dollop of sour cream and some crusty bread.

Borscht is a traditional soup originating from the Eastern European cuisine, specifically from Ukraine. The soup is typically made with beets, cabbage, and other vegetables, and can be served hot or cold. The combination of beets, vinegar, and sugar give the soup its signature sweet and sour flavor.

Ingredients:

- 2 tbsp olive oil
- 1 large onion, chopped
- 2 cloves garlic, minced
- 2 large potatoes, peeled and diced
- 2 cups fish stock
- 2 cups tomato sauce
- 1 tsp dried thyme
- Salt and pepper, to taste
- 2 lbs mixed seafood (shrimp, cod, clams, etc)
- 1 lemon, cut into wedges

Instructions:

1. In a large soup pot, heat the olive oil over medium heat.
2. Add the chopped onion and minced garlic, and cook until softened, about 5 minutes.
3. Add the diced potatoes, fish stock, tomato sauce, and dried thyme.
4. Bring the soup to a boil, then reduce heat and let it simmer for 10 minutes.
5. Season with salt and pepper to taste.
6. Add the mixed seafood to the soup and let it cook for another 5 minutes, until the seafood is fully cooked.

7. Serve hot with lemon wedges on the side.

Bouillabaisse is a traditional fish soup originating from the coastal city of Marseille, France. It is made with a mixture of various fish and shellfish, as well as vegetables such as leeks, potatoes, and tomatoes. The dish has a long history, with roots dating back to the 18th century, and it has become a staple of French Mediterranean cuisine.

Cullen Skink Soup

Ingredients:

- 2 lbs potatoes, peeled and diced
- 2 lbs smoked haddock
- 2 onions, chopped
- 1 cup of heavy cream
- 2 cloves of garlic, minced
- 2 tbsp butter
- Salt and pepper to taste

Instructions:

1. n a large saucepan, heat the butter over medium heat and add the chopped onions, cooking until they are soft and translucent.

2. Add the diced potatoes and minced garlic, and cook for a few minutes until fragrant.

3. Pour in enough water to cover the ingredients and bring to a boil. Reduce the heat and let simmer for 20 minutes or until the potatoes are tender.

4. Add the smoked haddock to the pan and cook for another 5-10 minutes, until the fish is cooked through.

5. Remove the saucepan from heat and blend the ingredients until smooth with a hand blender.

6. Stir in the heavy cream and season with salt and pepper to taste.

7. Serve hot with crusty bread.

Cullen Skink originates from Scotland and is a traditional Scottish soup made with smoked haddock and potatoes.

Erwtensoep (Dutch Pea Soup)

Ingredients:

- 2 lbs dried green split peas
- 8 cups of water
- 2 bay leaves
- 2 medium onions, chopped
- 2 carrots, chopped

- 2 stalks of celery, chopped

- 2 smoked ham hocks

- Salt and pepper to taste

Instructions:

1. Rinse the split peas and place in a large pot with the bay leaves and water.
2. Bring the water to a boil, then reduce the heat and let simmer for 1 hour or until the peas are soft.
3. In another pan, sauté the chopped onions, carrots, and celery until they are soft.
4. Add the sautéed vegetables and smoked ham hocks to the split peas and let cook for another hour.
5. Remove the ham hocks from the pot and let cool. Remove any meat from the bones and chop into small pieces.
6. Add the chopped ham back into the pot and blend the soup with a hand blender until smooth.
7. Season with salt and pepper to taste and serve hot.

Erwtensoep is a traditional Dutch soup made with green split peas and various meats and vegetables. It is typically eaten during the winter months.

Ingredients:

- 4 large potatoes, peeled and diced
- 2 large carrots, peeled and diced
- 1 large onion, diced
- 4 cups chicken or vegetable broth
- 2 cups heavy cream
- Salt and pepper to taste
- Fresh parsley for garnish

Instructions:

1. In a large pot, heat the diced onion and carrot until softened.
2. Add the diced potatoes and broth, then bring to a boil.
3. Reduce heat to a simmer and cook for 15-20 minutes or until the vegetables are soft.
4. Use an immersion blender to blend the soup until smooth.
5. Stir in the heavy cream, salt, and pepper.
6. Serve with fresh parsley.

This creamy soup originates from Ireland and is a popular comfort food in many countries.

Ingredients:

- 1 large head of escarole, chopped
- 1 large onion, diced
- 4 cups chicken or vegetable broth
- 2 cups water
- 1 can of cannellini beans, drained and rinsed
- Salt and pepper to taste
- Grated Parmesan cheese for garnish

Instructions:

1. In a large pot, heat the diced onion until softened.
2. Add the chopped escarole, broth, water, and cannellini beans.
3. Bring to a boil and then reduce heat to a simmer.
4. Cook for 15-20 minutes or until the escarole is tender.
5. Season with salt and pepper to taste.
6. Serve with grated Parmesan cheese.

This flavorful soup originates from Italy and is commonly enjoyed as a warm and comforting dish.

Ingredients:

- 2 cups green peas
- 2 medium carrots, peeled and diced
- 2 celery stalks, diced
- 1 large onion, diced
- 4 cups chicken or vegetable broth
- 2 cups water
- Salt and pepper to taste
- Fresh mint for garnish

Instructions:

1. In a large pot, heat the diced onion, carrot, and celery until softened.
2. Add the green peas, broth, and water, then bring to a boil.
3. Reduce heat to a simmer and cook for 20-25 minutes or until the vegetables are soft.
4. Use an immersion blender to blend the soup until smooth.
5. Season with salt and pepper to taste.
6. Serve with fresh mint.

This light and fresh soup is popular in many countries and is often enjoyed in the spring and summer.

Ingredients:

- 4 medium beets, peeled and diced
- 1 can of coconut milk
- 4 cups vegetable broth
- 1 large onion, diced
- Salt and pepper to taste
- Fresh cilantro for garnish

Instructions:

1. In a large pot, heat the diced onion until softened.
2. Add the diced beets, coconut milk, and vegetable broth.
3. Bring to a boil and then reduce heat to a simmer.
4. Cook for 20-25 minutes or until the beets are tender.
5. Use an immersion blender to blend the soup until smooth.
6. Season with salt and pepper to taste.
7. Serve with fresh cilantro.

This sweet and savory soup is popular in many Southeast Asian countries and is often enjoyed as a healthy and flavorful dish.

Ingredients:

- 2 dozen clams, chopped
- 2 cups of potatoes, diced
- 1 large onion, diced
- 4 cups fish broth
- 1 cup of heavy cream
- Salt and pepper to taste
- Fresh parsley for garnish

Instructions:

1. In a large pot, heat the diced onion until softened.
2. Add the diced potatoes, fish broth, and clams.
3. Bring to a boil and then reduce heat to a simmer.
4. Cook for 15-20 minutes or until the potatoes are tender.
5. Stir in the heavy cream.
6. Season with salt and pepper to taste.
7. Serve with fresh parsley.

This hearty and flavorful soup is a staple of coastal cuisine in the Pacific Northwest, known for its use of fresh clams and rich cream.

Ingredients:

- 2 cups carrots, diced
- 2 cups celery, diced
- 2 cups onions, diced
- 2 cups potatoes, diced
- 4 cups vegetable broth
- 2 cups water
- Salt and pepper to taste
- Fresh parsley for garnish

Instructions:

1. In a large pot, heat the diced onions until softened.
2. Add the diced carrots, celery, potatoes, broth, and water.
3. Bring to a boil and then reduce heat to a simmer.
4. Cook for 20-25 minutes or until the vegetables are tender.
5. Season with salt and pepper to taste.
6. Serve with fresh parsley.

This classic soup is a staple of American cuisine and is known for its simple and comforting flavors.

Ingredients:

- 2 cups mushrooms, sliced
- 1 cup pearl barley
- 1 large onion, diced
- 4 cups chicken or vegetable broth
- 2 cups water
- Salt and pepper to taste
- Fresh parsley for garnish

Instructions:

1. In a large pot, heat the diced onion until softened.
2. Add the sliced mushrooms, barley, broth, and water.
3. Bring to a boil and then reduce heat to a simmer.
4. Cook for 20-25 minutes or until the barley is tender.
5. Season with salt and pepper to taste.
6. Serve with fresh parsley.

This earthy and satisfying soup is popular in many countries and is often enjoyed as a warm and nourishing dish.

Ingredients:

- 1 lb boneless chicken breast, cubed
- 1 large onion, diced
- 4 carrots, peeled and diced
- 4 celery stalks, diced
- 4 garlic cloves, minced
- 4 cups chicken broth
- 2 cups water
- 1 tsp dried thyme
- 1 tsp dried rosemary
- 1 tsp dried basil
- Salt and pepper, to taste
- 2 cups all-purpose flour
- 1 tsp baking powder
- 1/2 tsp salt
- 1/4 cup unsalted butter
- 3/4 cup whole milk

Instructions:

1. In a large pot, cook the chicken over medium heat until browned.
2. Add the onion, carrots, celery, and garlic to the pot and cook until the vegetables are tender.

3. Stir in the chicken broth, water, thyme, rosemary, basil, salt, and pepper. Bring to a boil.

4. In a separate bowl, whisk together the flour, baking powder, and salt. Cut in the butter until the mixture resembles coarse crumbs.

5. Stir in the milk to form a soft dough. Drop spoonfuls of the dough into the boiling soup.

6. Cover the pot and simmer until the dumplings are cooked through, about 10 minutes.

The origin of Chicken and Dumpling Stew is unclear, but it is believed to have originated in the United States, particularly in the Southern states. Dumplings, which are small pieces of dough that are boiled or steamed, have been a staple food in various cultures for centuries, and it is likely that the combination of chicken and dumplings in stew form developed as a simple and satisfying way to use up ingredients that were readily available.

Zuppa di Tortellini

Ingredients:

- 8 cups chicken broth
- 1 cup heavy cream
- 1 onion, diced
- 4 garlic cloves, minced
- 2 cups fresh spinach, chopped

- 1 cup fresh basil, chopped

- 1 package (9 oz) cheese tortellini

- Salt and pepper, to taste

Instructions:

1. In a large pot, bring the chicken broth, heavy cream, onion, and garlic to a boil.
2. Add the spinach, basil, tortellini, salt, and pepper. Cook until the tortellini is al dente.
3. Serve hot.

The origin of Tortellini Soup is believed to be in the Emilia-Romagna region of Italy, where tortellini is a traditional filled pasta. The dish is thought to have originated as a way to use leftover tortellini, which would be added to a broth to make a simple and satisfying meal.

Spinach and Chickpea Soup

Ingredients:

- 2 tbsp olive oil

- 1 onion, diced

- 4 garlic cloves, minced
- 4 cups chicken broth
- 2 cans chickpeas, drained and rinsed
- 4 cups fresh spinach
- 1 tsp dried basil
- Salt and pepper, to taste

Instructions:

1. In a large pot, heat the olive oil over medium heat. Add the onion and garlic and cook until softened.
2. Stir in the chicken broth, chickpeas, spinach, basil, salt, and pepper. Bring to a boil.
3. Reduce heat to low and simmer for 10 minutes.
4. Serve hot.

The origin of Spinach and Chickpea Soup is difficult to trace, as it is a dish that has likely been enjoyed in various cultures for centuries. Chickpeas, also known as garbanzo beans, have been a staple food in the Mediterranean region for thousands of years and are still widely used in Middle Eastern and Mediterranean cuisines. Spinach, on the other hand, is believed to have originated in Iran and was later introduced to Europe in the 10th century.

East Coast Clam Chowder

Ingredients:

- 6 slices of bacon, diced
- 1 large onion, chopped
- 3 cloves of garlic, minced
- 3 large potatoes, peeled and diced
- 3 cups of water
- 3 cups of milk
- 2 cans of minced clams
- Salt and pepper to taste
- Parsley, chopped, for garnish

Instructions:

1. In a large saucepan, cook the bacon over medium heat until crispy.
2. Add the onion and garlic and cook until softened, about 5 minutes.
3. Add the potatoes, water, milk, and clams to the saucepan and bring to a boil.
4. Reduce heat and simmer for about 20 minutes, or until the potatoes are tender.
5. Season with salt and pepper to taste.
6. Serve hot, garnished with parsley.

Origins: Clam chowder is a traditional New England dish that has been a staple for generations. It is believed to have been created by early settlers who used clams and potatoes to make a hearty and filling soup.

Pumpkin Stew

Ingredients:

- 1 large onion, chopped
- 3 cloves of garlic, minced
- 1 large pumpkin, peeled and diced
- 3 cups of chicken broth
- 2 cups of coconut milk
- Salt and pepper to taste
- Fresh cilantro, chopped, for garnish

Instructions:

1. In a large saucepan, cook the onion and garlic over medium heat until softened, about 5 minutes.
2. Add the pumpkin and chicken broth to the saucepan and bring to a boil.
3. Reduce heat and simmer for about 20 minutes, or until the pumpkin is tender.

4. Stir in the coconut milk and season with salt and pepper to taste.

5. Serve hot, garnished with cilantro.

Origins: Pumpkin stew is a popular dish in many cultures and is often served as a comforting and warming meal. It can be traced back to ancient civilizations who used pumpkin as a staple ingredient in their cooking.

Matzo Ball Stew

Ingredients:

- 6 cups of chicken broth
- 3 carrots, chopped
- 3 celery stalks, chopped
- 1 large onion, chopped
- 2 cloves of garlic, minced
- 2 cups of matzo balls (homemade or store-bought)
- Salt and pepper to taste
- Fresh parsley, chopped, for garnish

Instructions:

1. In a large saucepan, bring the chicken broth to a boil.
2. Add the carrots, celery, onion, and garlic and cook until softened, about 10 minutes.

3. Add the matzo balls to the saucepan and simmer for about 10 minutes.
4. Season with salt and pepper to taste.
5. Serve hot, garnished with parsley.

Origins: Matzo ball stew is a traditional Jewish dish that is often served during holidays such as Passover. The matzo balls, made from matzo meal, symbolize the unleavened bread that was eaten by the Israelites during their exodus from Egypt.

Beef Pho Soup

Ingredients:

- Beef bones
- Star anise
- Cinnamon sticks
- Cloves
- Ginger
- Onions
- Rice noodles
- Beef sirloin
- Bean sprouts
- Fresh basil

- Fresh cilantro

- Lime

- Hoisin sauce

- Sriracha sauce

- Salt

- Black pepper

Instructions:

1. Boil beef bones in a large pot of water for 2 hours.
2. Add star anise, cinnamon sticks, cloves, ginger, and onions to the pot and simmer for another hour.
3. Strain the broth and discard the solids.
4. Cook the rice noodles according to the package instructions.
5. Slice the beef sirloin thinly.
6. Divide the noodles into bowls, add the beef and bean sprouts on top.
7. Pour hot broth over the noodles and beef.
8. Serve with fresh basil, cilantro, lime, hoisin sauce, sriracha sauce, salt, and black pepper.

Origins: Pho is a popular Vietnamese noodle soup that originated in northern Vietnam in the early 20th century.

Ingredients:

- Butter
- Onions
- Garlic
- Flour
- Chicken broth
- Beer
- Milk
- Cheddar cheese
- Salt
- Black pepper

Instructions:

1. Melt butter in a large pot over medium heat.
2. Add onions and garlic and cook until soft.
3. Add flour and cook, stirring constantly, for 2 minutes.
4. Gradually add chicken broth, beer, and milk, stirring constantly.
5. Bring to a boil, then reduce heat and let simmer for 10 minutes.
6. Stir in cheddar cheese until melted.
7. Season with salt and black pepper to taste.
8. Serve hot.

Origins: Beer and cheddar soup is a traditional soup from the American Midwest, particularly Wisconsin, where beer and cheese are both produced.

Ingredients:

- Olive oil
- Onions
- Garlic
- Tomatoes
- Red pepper flakes
- Paprika
- Cumin
- Salt
- Black pepper
- Potatoes
- Shrimp
- Chicken broth
- Lemon juice
- Fresh cilantro

Instructions:

1. Heat olive oil in a large pot over medium heat.
2. Add onions and garlic and cook until soft.
3. Add tomatoes, red pepper flakes, paprika, cumin, salt, and black pepper to the pot.
4. Cook for 5 minutes, stirring occasionally.
5. Add potatoes, shrimp, and chicken broth to the pot.
6. Bring to a boil, then reduce heat and let simmer for 10 minutes.
7. Stir in lemon juice and cilantro.
8. Serve hot.

Origins: This spicy shrimp stew is a fusion of various cuisines, with ingredients and spices common in both Mediterranean and Latin American cooking.

Crab Bisque

Ingredients:

- Butter
- Onion
- Garlic
- Flour
- White wine
- Chicken broth

- Heavy cream
- Crab meat
- Salt
- Black pepper
- Paprika

Instructions:

1. Melt butter in a large pot over medium heat.
2. Add onion and garlic and cook until soft.
3. Add flour and cook, stirring constantly, for 2 minutes.
4. Gradually add white wine, chicken broth, and heavy cream, stirring constantly.
5. Bring to a boil, then reduce heat and let simmer for 10 minutes.
6. Stir in crab meat and season with salt, black pepper, and paprika to taste.
7. Serve hot.

Origins: Crab bisque is a classic French soup that originated in the coastal regions of France, where crab is a common ingredient in cooking.

Ingredients:

- Olive oil
- Onions
- Garlic
- Beets
- Tomatoes
- Chicken broth
- Balsamic vinegar
- Salt
- Black pepper

Instructions:

1. Heat olive oil in a large pot over medium heat.
2. Add onions and garlic and cook until soft.
3. Add beets and tomatoes to the pot and cook for 5 minutes.
4. Pour in chicken broth and bring to a boil.
5. Reduce heat and let simmer for 20 minutes.
6. Puree the soup with an immersion blender or transfer to a blender and blend until smooth.
7. Stir in balsamic vinegar and season with salt and black pepper to taste.
8. Serve hot.

Origins: This beet and tomato soup is a simple, healthy, and delicious combination of ingredients that can be found in many different cuisines around the world.

Potato and Asparagus Soup

Ingredients:

- Olive oil
- Onions
- Garlic
- Potatoes
- Asparagus
- Chicken broth
- Heavy cream
- Salt
- Black pepper

Instructions:

1. Heat olive oil in a large pot over medium heat.
2. Add onions and garlic and cook until soft.
3. Add potatoes and asparagus to the pot and cook for 5 minutes.
4. Pour in chicken broth and bring to a boil.
5. Reduce heat and let simmer for 20 minutes.

6. Puree the soup with an immersion blender or transfer to a blender and blend until smooth.

7. Stir in heavy cream and season with salt and black pepper to taste.

8. Serve hot.

Origins: This potato and asparagus soup is a comforting and satisfying dish that is popular in many different cuisines and can be found in many different variations around the world.

Oyster Stew

Ingredients:

- Butter
- Onion
- Garlic
- Flour
- Milk
- Oysters
- Salt
- Black pepper

Instructions:

1. Melt butter in a large pot over medium heat.

2. Add onion and garlic and cook until soft.

3. Add flour and cook, stirring constantly, for 2 minutes.

4. Gradually add milk, stirring constantly, until mixture thickens.

5. Stir in oysters and season with salt and black pepper to taste.

6. Cook until oysters are heated through, about 5 minutes.

7. Serve hot.

Origins: Oyster stew is a classic American dish that originated on the East Coast, where oysters were abundant and a staple food of many coastal communities.

Green Chili Pork Stew

Ingredients:

- Olive oil
- Pork shoulder
- Onions
- Garlic
- Green chilies
- Tomatoes
- Chicken broth
- Cilantro
- Salt
- Black pepper

Instructions:

1. Heat olive oil in a large pot over medium heat.
2. Add pork shoulder and cook until browned on all sides.
3. Add onions and garlic and cook until soft.
4. Stir in green chilies, tomatoes, and chicken broth.
5. Bring to a boil, then reduce heat and let simmer for 30 minutes.
6. Stir in cilantro and season with salt and black pepper to taste.
7. Serve hot.

Origins: Green chili pork stew is a traditional Mexican dish that combines spicy green chilies with tender pork shoulder and a variety of other flavorful ingredients.

Cheeseburger Soup

Ingredients:

- Butter
- Onion
- Garlic
- Ground beef
- Flour
- Chicken broth

- Milk
- Cheddar cheese
- Salt
- Black pepper
- Paprika
- Crushed crackers (optional)

Instructions:

1. Melt butter in a large pot over medium heat.
2. Add onion and garlic and cook until soft.
3. Add ground beef and cook until browned.
4. Add flour and cook, stirring constantly, for 2 minutes.
5. Gradually add chicken broth and milk, stirring constantly, until mixture thickens.
6. Stir in cheddar cheese until melted.
7. Season with salt, black pepper, and paprika to taste.
8. Serve hot, topped with crushed crackers if desired.

Origins: Cheeseburger soup is a classic American dish that takes the flavors of a juicy cheeseburger and transforms them into a hearty and satisfying soup.

Ingredients:

- 4 boneless chicken breasts, cut into 1-inch cubes
- 2 tablespoons olive oil
- 1 onion, chopped
- 2 cloves garlic, minced
- 2 celery stalks, diced
- 2 carrots, peeled and diced
- 2 tablespoons flour
- 4 cups chicken broth
- 1 cup Frank's RedHot sauce
- 1/2 cup blue cheese dressing
- Salt and pepper to taste

Instructions:

1. In a large pot, heat the olive oil over medium heat. Add the chicken and cook until browned, about 5 minutes.
2. Add the onion, garlic, celery, and carrots and cook for an additional 5 minutes, until the vegetables are soft.
3. Sprinkle the flour over the vegetables and chicken and stir to combine.
4. Gradually add the chicken broth, stirring constantly to prevent lumps from forming.

5. Stir in the hot sauce and blue cheese dressing and season with salt and pepper to taste.

6. Simmer for 10-15 minutes, until the soup has thickened slightly and the chicken is cooked through.

Buffalo chicken soup is a spicy, hearty soup that is perfect for cold winter days. Its origin can be traced back to Buffalo, New York, where it is said to have been created to mimic the flavors of Buffalo chicken wings.

Sweet Potato Chowder

Ingredients:

- 2 tablespoons butter
- 1 onion, chopped
- 2 cloves garlic, minced
- 2 large sweet potatoes, peeled and diced
- 4 cups chicken broth
- 1 cup heavy cream
- Salt and pepper to taste
- Chopped fresh parsley, for garnish

Instructions:

1. In a large pot, melt the butter over medium heat. Add the onion and garlic and cook until soft, about 5 minutes.
2. Add the sweet potatoes and chicken broth and bring to a boil.
3. Reduce heat to low and simmer for 20-30 minutes, until the sweet potatoes are soft.
4. Use an immersion blender or transfer the soup to a blender and puree until smooth.
5. Stir in the heavy cream and season with salt and pepper to taste.
6. Serve hot, garnished with chopped parsley.

Sweet potato chowder is a creamy, comforting soup that is perfect for fall. Its origin is not clear, but it likely evolved from traditional potato chowder recipes.

Spinach Bisque

Ingredients:

- 2 tablespoons butter
- 1 onion, chopped
- 2 cloves garlic, minced
- 5 cups chicken broth
- 2 cups chopped spinach
- 1 cup heavy cream

- Salt and pepper to taste

- Croutons, for garnish

Instructions:

1. In a large pot, melt the butter over medium heat. Add the onion and garlic and cook until soft, about 5 minutes.
2. Add the chicken broth and spinach and bring to a boil.
3. Reduce heat to low and simmer for 10-15 minutes, until the spinach is soft.
4. Use an immersion blender or transfer the soup to a blender and puree until smooth.
5. Stir in the heavy cream and season with salt and pepper to taste.
6. Serve hot, garnished with croutons.

Spinach bisque is a creamy, flavorful soup that is perfect for a light lunch or dinner. Its origin is not clear, but it likely evolved from traditional spinach soup recipes.

Ingredients:

- 4 boneless, skinless chicken breasts, cut into small pieces
- 2 large onions, chopped
- 2 large bell peppers, chopped
- 1 large stalk celery, chopped
- 1 teaspoon dried thyme
- 1 teaspoon dried basil
- 1/2 teaspoon cayenne pepper
- 4 cloves garlic, minced
- 3 tablespoons all-purpose flour
- 4 cups chicken broth
- 2 cups canned diced tomatoes
- 2 cups sliced okra
- Salt and pepper, to taste

Instructions:

1. In a large pot, heat oil over medium heat.
2. Add chicken and cook until browned, about 5 minutes.
3. Add onions, peppers, celery, thyme, basil, cayenne, and garlic to the pot. Cook until vegetables are tender, about 5 minutes.
4. Stir in flour and cook for 2 minutes.
5. Gradually whisk in chicken broth and diced tomatoes.
6. Stir in okra and season with salt and pepper.

7. Bring to a boil, then reduce heat and simmer for 30 minutes.

Chicken gumbo is a stew that originated in Louisiana and combines ingredients and cooking techniques from West African, French, Spanish, and Native American cultures.

Chicken Ravioli Soup

Ingredients:

- 1 (9 oz) package fresh chicken ravioli
- 4 cups chicken broth
- 2 cups chopped spinach
- 1 can diced tomatoes
- 2 cloves garlic, minced
- Salt and pepper, to taste

Instructions:

1. In a large pot, heat chicken broth over medium heat.
2. Add ravioli and cook until tender, about 5 minutes.
3. Stir in spinach, tomatoes, and garlic.
4. Season with salt and pepper.
5. Cook until heated through, about 5 minutes.

Chicken ravioli soup is a comforting and easy-to-make soup that is perfect for a quick lunch or dinner.

Hearty Cabbage Soup

Ingredients:

- 1 large head cabbage, chopped
- 2 large carrots, chopped
- 2 large onions, chopped
- 2 cloves garlic, minced
- 4 cups beef broth
- 1 can diced tomatoes
- 2 teaspoons dried basil
- Salt and pepper, to taste

Instructions:

1. In a large pot, heat oil over medium heat.
2. Add cabbage, carrots, onions, and garlic to the pot. Cook until vegetables are tender, about 10 minutes.
3. Stir in beef broth, diced tomatoes, and basil.
4. Season with salt and pepper.
5. Bring to a boil, then reduce heat and simmer for 30 minutes.

Cabbage soup is a classic dish that is enjoyed all over the world and is a staple in many cultures. It is simple, filling, and a great way to get your daily dose of vegetables.

Ingredients:

- 4 cups fresh corn kernels (about 4 ears)
- 2 cups chicken broth
- 1 cup heavy cream
- 2 tablespoons honey
- Salt and pepper, to taste
- Fresh chives, chopped, for garnish

Instructions:

1. In a large pot, combine corn kernels and chicken broth.
2. Bring to a boil, then reduce heat and simmer for 15 minutes.
3. Remove from heat and let cool for 10 minutes.
4. Blend the mixture in a blender until smooth.
5. Return the mixture to the pot and add heavy cream and honey.
6. Season with salt and pepper.
7. Cook until heated through, about 5 minutes.

8. Serve hot and garnish with chives.

Sweet and savory corn soup is a classic summer soup that takes advantage of the sweet and juicy corn that is in season. It is a simple, comforting, and delicious soup that is perfect for a hot summer day.

Easy Tomato Gnocchi Soup

Ingredients:

- 1 (16 oz) package fresh gnocchi
- 4 cups chicken broth
- 2 cups canned diced tomatoes
- 2 cloves garlic, minced
- Salt and pepper, to taste
- Fresh basil, chopped, for garnish

Instructions:

1. In a large pot, heat chicken broth over medium heat.
2. Add gnocchi and cook until tender, about 5 minutes.
3. Stir in diced tomatoes and garlic.
4. Season with salt and pepper.
5. Cook until heated through, about 5 minutes.
6. Serve hot and garnish with basil.

Tomato gnocchi soup is a classic Italian soup that is both comforting and easy to make. The tender gnocchi and the juicy, flavorful tomatoes make this soup a crowd-pleaser.

Roasted Pepper Soup

Ingredients:

- 4 red bell peppers, roasted and chopped
- 2 large onions, chopped
- 2 cloves garlic, minced
- 4 cups chicken broth
- 1 can diced tomatoes
- Salt and pepper, to taste
- Fresh cilantro, chopped, for garnish

Instructions:

1. In a large pot, heat oil over medium heat.
2. Add onions and garlic to the pot. Cook until tender, about 5 minutes.
3. Stir in roasted red peppers, chicken broth, and diced tomatoes.
4. Season with salt and pepper.
5. Bring to a boil, then reduce heat and simmer for 15 minutes.

6. Blend the mixture in a blender until smooth.

7. Return the mixture to the pot and cook until heated through, about 5 minutes.

8. Serve hot and garnish with cilantro.

Roasted pepper soup is a delicious and healthy soup that takes advantage of the sweet, smoky flavor of roasted peppers. It is a simple and easy-to-make soup that is perfect for a light lunch or dinner.

Ginger Apple Carrot Soup

Ingredients:

- 4 medium carrots, peeled and chopped
- 2 medium apples, peeled and chopped
- 1 inch ginger root, peeled and chopped
- 2 cloves of garlic, minced
- 2 cups chicken or vegetable broth
- 1 cup heavy cream
- Salt and pepper to taste

Instructions:

1. In a large pot, heat a tablespoon of oil over medium heat.

2. Add the ginger, garlic, and carrots to the pot and cook until they begin to soften, about 5 minutes.

3. Add the apples and broth to the pot, bring to a boil and then reduce heat to low.

4. Simmer for 20 minutes or until the carrots are tender.

5. Remove from heat and blend with an immersion blender or transfer to a blender and puree until smooth.

6. Stir in the heavy cream and season with salt and pepper to taste.

7. Reheat on low heat until warmed through.

The origin of Ginger Apple Carrot Soup is not clear, but it is likely a modern take on traditional vegetable soups. Carrots, apples, and ginger have long been used in cooking and are popular ingredients in many cuisines.

Coconut Pumpkin Soup

Ingredients:

- 1 small pumpkin, peeled, seeded, and chopped
- 1 can coconut milk
- 1 onion, chopped
- 2 cloves of garlic, minced
- 2 cups chicken or vegetable broth
- Salt and pepper to taste

Instructions:

1. In a large pot, heat a tablespoon of oil over medium heat.
2. Add the onion and garlic to the pot and cook until they begin to soften, about 5 minutes.
3. Add the pumpkin, broth, and coconut milk to the pot, bring to a boil and then reduce heat to low.
4. Simmer for 20 minutes or until the pumpkin is tender.
5. Remove from heat and blend with an immersion blender or transfer to a blender and puree until smooth.
6. Season with salt and pepper to taste.
7. Reheat on low heat until warmed through.

The origin of Coconut Pumpkin Soup is not clear, but it is likely a fusion of traditional pumpkin soups and dishes from Southeast Asian cuisine that utilize coconut milk. Pumpkin is a staple ingredient in many cultures, and its sweet and creamy flesh has been used in soups for centuries.

Creamy Celery Soup

Ingredients:

- 4 stalks of celery, chopped
- 1 onion, chopped
- 2 cloves of garlic, minced
- 2 cups chicken or vegetable broth
- 1 cup heavy cream
- Salt and pepper to taste

Instructions:

1. In a large pot, heat a tablespoon of oil over medium heat.
2. Add the onion, garlic, and celery to the pot and cook until they begin to soften, about 5 minutes.
3. Add the broth to the pot, bring to a boil and then reduce heat to low.
4. Simmer for 20 minutes or until the celery is tender.
5. Remove from heat and blend with an immersion blender or transfer to a blender and puree until smooth.

6. Stir in the heavy cream and season with salt and pepper to taste.

7. Reheat on low heat until warmed through.

The origin of Creamy Celery Soup is not well documented, but it is likely a variation of traditional vegetable soups that have been popular for centuries. Celery has been used in cooking for a long time, and it is likely that at some point, someone combined celery with cream to create a creamy and comforting soup.

Tuscan Chicken Soup

Ingredients:

- 2 tablespoons olive oil
- 1 onion, diced
- 2 garlic cloves, minced
- 4 boneless chicken breasts, cut into bite-sized pieces
- 2 cans of diced tomatoes
- 4 cups chicken broth
- 1 cup heavy cream
- Salt and pepper to taste
- Fresh basil, chopped
-

Instructions:

1. In a large pot, heat the olive oil over medium heat.
2. Add the onion and garlic and cook until the onion is soft and translucent.
3. Add the chicken to the pot and cook until browned.
4. Pour in the diced tomatoes and chicken broth.
5. Bring the mixture to a boil, then reduce the heat and let it simmer for 20-30 minutes.
6. Stir in the heavy cream and let it simmer for an additional 5 minutes.
7. Season with salt and pepper to taste.
8. Serve hot with fresh basil on top.

Tuscan chicken soup is a traditional Italian soup that is rich and hearty.

Polish Chicken Broth

Ingredients:

- 1 whole chicken
- 1 onion, sliced
- 2 carrots, sliced
- 2 celery stalks, sliced

- 4 cups chicken broth

- 2 cups water

- Salt and pepper to taste

Instructions:

1. In a large pot, place the whole chicken, onion, carrots, celery.

2. Pour in the chicken broth and water.

3. Bring the mixture to a boil, then reduce the heat and let it simmer for 2 hours.

4. Strain the broth and season with salt and pepper to taste.

5. Serve hot.

Polish chicken broth is a classic soup that is simple and nourishing.

Chicken Lentil Soup

Ingredients:

- 2 tablespoons olive oil

- 1 onion, diced

- 2 garlic cloves, minced

- 2 boneless chicken breasts, cut into bite-sized pieces

- 1 cup green lentils, rinsed

- 4 cups chicken broth

- 1 can of diced tomatoes

- Salt and pepper to taste

Instructions:

1. In a large pot, heat the olive oil over medium heat.
2. Add the onion and garlic and cook until the onion is soft and translucent.
3. Add the chicken to the pot and cook until browned.
4. Pour in the diced tomatoes, chicken broth, and green lentils.
5. Bring the mixture to a boil, then reduce the heat and let it simmer for 30 minutes.
6. Season with salt and pepper to taste.
7. Serve hot.

Chicken lentil soup is a hearty and nutritious soup that is popular in many cultures.

California Vegetable Medley Soup

Ingredients:

- 2 tablespoons olive oil
- 1 onion, diced
- 2 garlic cloves, minced
- 2 carrots, chopped
- 2 celery stalks, chopped
- 2 zucchini, chopped
- 2 bell peppers, chopped
- 4 cups vegetable broth
- 1 can of diced tomatoes
- Salt and pepper to taste
- Fresh basil, chopped

Instructions:

1. In a large pot, heat the olive oil over medium heat.
2. Add the onion and garlic and cook until the onion is soft and translucent.
3. Add the carrots, celery, zucchini, and bell peppers to the pot.
4. Pour in the vegetable broth and diced tomatoes.
5. Bring the mixture to a boil, then reduce the heat and let it simmer for 20-30 minutes.
6. Season with salt and pepper to taste.
7. Serve hot with fresh basil on top.

California vegetable medley soup is a healthy and flavorful soup that is inspired by the fresh ingredients found in California.

Mediterranean Vegetable Soup

Ingredients:

- 2 tablespoons olive oil
- 1 onion, diced
- 2 garlic cloves, minced
- 2 carrots, chopped
- 2 celery stalks, chopped
- 2 zucchini, chopped
- 2 bell peppers, chopped
- 1 can of chickpeas, drained
- 4 cups vegetable broth
- Salt and pepper to taste
- Fresh parsley, chopped

Instructions:

1. In a large pot, heat the olive oil over medium heat.
2. Add the onion and garlic and cook until the onion is soft and translucent.

3. Add the carrots, celery, zucchini, and bell peppers to the pot.

4. Pour in the chickpeas and vegetable broth.

5. Bring the mixture to a boil, then reduce the heat and let it simmer for 20-30 minutes.

6. Season with salt and pepper to taste.

7. Serve hot with fresh parsley on top.

Mediterranean vegetable soup is a healthy and flavorful soup that is inspired by the fresh ingredients found in the Mediterranean.

North African Vegetable Soup

Ingredients:

- 2 tablespoons olive oil
- 1 onion, diced
- 2 garlic cloves, minced
- 2 carrots, chopped
- 2 celery stalks, chopped
- 2 zucchini, chopped
- 1 can of chickpeas, drained
- 4 cups vegetable broth
- 1 teaspoon cumin
- 1 teaspoon paprika

- Salt and pepper to taste
- Fresh cilantro, chopped

Instructions:

1. In a large pot, heat the olive oil over medium heat.
2. Add the onion and garlic and cook until the onion is soft and translucent.
3. Add the carrots, celery, zucchini, and chickpeas to the pot.
4. Pour in the vegetable broth.
5. Sprinkle in the cumin and paprika.
6. Bring the mixture to a boil, then reduce the heat and let it simmer for 20-30 minutes.
7. Season with salt and pepper to taste.
8. Serve hot with fresh cilantro on top.

North African vegetable soup is a healthy and flavorful soup that is inspired by the spices and ingredients found in North Africa.

Indonesian Crab Soup

Ingredients:

- 2 lbs crab meat
- 2 tablespoons oil

- 1 large onion, diced
- 3 cloves garlic, minced
- 2 tablespoons ginger, minced
- 2 red chilies, seeded and chopped
- 1 tablespoon ground coriander
- 1 teaspoon ground cumin
- 2 tablespoons tomato paste
- 4 cups chicken broth
- 2 tablespoons lemon juice
- Salt and pepper to taste

Instructions:

1. In a large pot, heat the oil over medium heat.
2. Add the onion, garlic, ginger, chilies, coriander and cumin, and cook until the onion is soft.
3. Stir in the tomato paste and cook for another 2 minutes.
4. Add the chicken broth and bring to a boil.
5. Add the crab meat and simmer for 10 minutes.
6. Stir in the lemon juice, season with salt and pepper to taste.
7. Serve hot.

This soup originates from Indonesia and is known for its rich, spicy and flavorful broth.

Pure Texas Beef Chili Soup

Ingredients:

- 2 lbs beef chuck, diced
- 2 tablespoons oil
- 1 large onion, diced
- 2 red bell peppers, diced
- 2 cloves garlic, minced
- 2 tablespoons chili powder
- 1 teaspoon ground cumin
- 1 teaspoon dried oregano
- 1 can (14.5 oz) diced tomatoes
- 4 cups beef broth
- Salt and pepper to taste

Instructions:

1. In a large pot, heat the oil over medium heat.
2. Add the beef and cook until browned.
3. Remove the beef and set aside.
4. Add the onion, bell pepper, garlic, chili powder, cumin and oregano to the pot, and cook until the onion is soft.
5. Return the beef to the pot, along with the diced tomatoes and beef broth.
6. Bring to a boil, then reduce the heat and simmer for 30 minutes.

7. Season with salt and pepper to taste.

8. Serve hot with your favorite toppings.

This hearty soup is a staple in Texas, where it is known for its bold and spicy flavors.

New England Clam Chowder

Ingredients:

- 2 lbs chopped clams
- 2 tablespoons butter
- 1 large onion, diced
- 2 celery stalks, diced
- 2 cloves garlic, minced
- 2 tablespoons flour
- 4 cups milk
- 2 cups potatoes, diced
- Salt and pepper to taste

Instructions:

1. In a large pot, heat the butter over medium heat.
2. Add the onion, celery and garlic, and cook until the onion is soft.
3. Stir in the flour and cook for another 2 minutes.

4. Gradually add the milk, stirring constantly, until the mixture comes to a boil.

5. Add the potatoes and clams, and simmer until the potatoes are tender.

6. Season with salt and pepper to taste.

7. Serve hot.

This creamy and delicious soup originates from the New England region of the United States and is a classic comfort food.

Gazpacho Soup

Ingredients:

- 4 large ripe tomatoes, peeled and chopped
- 1 cucumber, peeled and chopped
- 1 red bell pepper, chopped
- 1 red onion, chopped
- 2 cloves garlic, minced
- 2 tablespoons red wine vinegar
- 2 tablespoons olive oil
- Salt and pepper to taste
- Ice cubes

Instructions:

1. In a blender, combine the tomatoes, cucumber, bell pepper, onion, garlic, vinegar and oil.
2. Blend until smooth.
3. Season with salt and pepper to taste.
4. Chill in the refrigerator for at least 1 hour.
5. Serve cold with ice cubes and additional seasonings, if desired.

Gazpacho soup originates from Andalusia, Spain, and is a refreshing summer soup traditionally made with ripe, in-season vegetables.

Tom Yum Soup Recipe

Ingredients:

- 1 liter chicken broth
- 5 kaffir lime leaves
- 5-6 sliced lemongrass
- 5 sliced galangal
- 5 sliced shallots
- 4 sliced bird's eye chili
- 4 chopped garlic cloves
- 2 tablespoons fish sauce

- 2 tablespoons lime juice

- 2 tablespoons palm sugar

- 150g sliced mushrooms

- 100g prawns

- Fresh cilantro leaves for garnish

Instructions:

1. In a large pot, bring chicken broth to a boil.
2. Add kaffir lime leaves, lemongrass, galangal, shallots, chili, and garlic.
3. Reduce heat and let simmer for 10 minutes.
4. Add fish sauce, lime juice, palm sugar, mushrooms, and prawns.
5. Let cook for another 5 minutes.
6. Serve hot and garnish with cilantro leaves.

Tom Yum Soup originates from Thailand and is a hot and sour soup with a balance of flavors from chili, lemongrass, and lime juice.

Ingredients:

- 4 tablespoons butter
- 1 chopped onion
- 3 diced celery stalks
- 3 diced carrots
- 4 chopped garlic cloves
- 1/4 cup all-purpose flour
- 3 cups chicken broth
- 2 cups heavy cream
- 1 teaspoon Old Bay seasoning
- 1 teaspoon dried thyme
- Salt and pepper to taste
- 500g crab meat
- Fresh parsley for garnish

Instructions:

1. In a large pot, melt butter over medium heat.
2. Add onion, celery, carrots, and garlic. Cook until vegetables are soft.
3. Stir in flour to make a roux.
4. Gradually add chicken broth and cream, stirring constantly.
5. Add Old Bay seasoning, thyme, salt, and pepper.
6. Let simmer for 15 minutes.

7. Add crab meat and cook until heated through.

8. Serve hot and garnish with parsley.

Maryland Crab Chowder is a classic American chowder made with crab meat and a creamy base seasoned with Old Bay, a blend of herbs and spices originating from the Chesapeake Bay area.

Rouille Recipe

Ingredients:

- 3 cloves garlic
- 1/2 teaspoon salt
- 1 egg yolk
- 1/2 cup olive oil
- 2 tablespoons lemon juice
- 1/4 teaspoon cayenne pepper

Instructions:

1. Crush garlic and salt in a mortar and pestle.
2. In a mixing bowl, whisk together the garlic mixture and egg yolk.
3. Gradually drizzle in olive oil, whisking constantly.
4. Stir in lemon juice and cayenne pepper.
5. Serve with bread or as a sauce for soup.

Rouille is a garlic and olive oil sauce originating from the Provence region of France. It is commonly used as a condiment for soups such as bouillabaisse.

Vietnamese Pho with Beef Recipe

Ingredients:

- 1 onion
- 2 inch piece of ginger
- 1 cinnamon stick
- 3 whole star anise
- 3 cloves
- 6 cups beef broth
- 2 tablespoons fish sauce
- 1 tablespoon sugar
- 1 teaspoon salt
- 8 oz rice noodles
- 8 oz sirloin steak, thinly sliced
- Fresh basil leaves
- Fresh cilantro leaves
- Fresh bean sprouts
- Fresh lime wedges
- Hot sauce to taste

Instructions:

1. Cut onion in half and char over an open flame until blackened. Repeat with ginger.
2. In a large pot, add onion, ginger, cinnamon stick, star anise, cloves, beef broth, fish sauce, sugar, and salt. Let simmer for 30 minutes.
3. Strain the broth and discard solids.
4. Cook rice noodles according to package instructions.
5. In bowls, divide noodles and steak.
6. Ladle hot broth over noodles and steak.
7. Serve with basil, cilantro, bean sprouts, lime wedges, and hot sauce on the side.

Pho is a popular Vietnamese noodle soup dish made with a flavorful broth, rice noodles, and various meats. The origin of Pho can be traced back to the early 20th century in Northern Vietnam.

Sauerkraut Soup Recipe

Ingredients:

- 1 medium onion, chopped
- 2 tablespoons butter
- 2 pounds sauerkraut, drained and rinsed
- 6 cups chicken or vegetable broth
- 2 medium potatoes, peeled and diced
- 1 teaspoon caraway seeds

- 2 tablespoons sour cream (optional)

Instructions:

1. In a large saucepan, sauté the onion in the butter until soft.
2. Add the sauerkraut, broth, potatoes, and caraway seeds.
3. Simmer for 30 minutes, or until the potatoes are tender.
4. Serve with a dollop of sour cream on each bowl, if desired.

Note: Sauerkraut soup is a traditional dish in Central and Eastern European cuisine, particularly in Germany, Austria, and the Czech Republic.

Pearl Barley Soup Recipe

Ingredients:

- 1 medium onion, chopped
- 2 tablespoons olive oil
- 1 cup pearl barley
- 6 cups chicken or vegetable broth
- 2 carrots, peeled and diced
- 2 stalks celery, diced
- 1 teaspoon dried rosemary
- 2 tablespoons grated Parmesan cheese (optional)

Instructions:

1. In a large saucepan, sauté the onion in the oil until soft.
2. Add the barley, broth, carrots, celery, and rosemary.
3. Simmer for 30 minutes, or until the barley is tender.
4. Serve with a sprinkle of Parmesan cheese on each bowl, if desired.

Note: Pearl barley is a common ingredient in soups in many countries, including Italy, where it is used to add texture and heartiness to broths.

Conclusion

In conclusion, soups are a versatile and comforting dish that can be enjoyed all year round. With this recipe book, you now have a collection of delicious soup recipes to choose from, each with its own unique flavor and ingredients. Whether you prefer creamy, hearty, or light soups, there is something for everyone in this collection. So, gather your ingredients, heat up your pot, and start whipping up some soul-satisfying soups!